MAJESTY

PROMISES REVEALED IN THE NAMES OF GOD

THE NAMES OF GOD REVEAL HIS PERSON AND CHARACTER, AND HIS WORD REVEALS GOD AND HIS NAMES.

MAJESTY

ELOHIM
THE SOVEREIGN, MIGHTY CREATOR

In the beginning God created the heavens and the earth . . .

GENESIS 1:1 NLT

The very first name of God found in the Bible is *Elohim*, which means God the Creator. His creation displays His UNIMAGINABLE AND LIMITLESS POWER.

The Hebrew word for the name "God" is *El,* or *Elohim,* and this name is one of God's more frequently occurring titles—used more than 2500 times in the Bible! It is crucial to understand its meaning. *El* is the root word of *Elohim*, and it describes God's GREATNESS AND GLORY; it displays God's power and sovereignty in all things.

"LORD, the God of Israel, there is no God like you in heaven above or on earth below—you who keep your covenant of love with your servants who continue wholeheartedly in your way."

1 KINGS 8:23

God knows how to care and provide for His creation. He has done it from the very beginning. GOD IS ABLE to see you through any difficulty, EVEN A FLOOD! No matter what the circumstances in your life might be, *Elohim* desires to renew your spirit, mind, body, emotions and image. God longs for you to rely on Him as your Source of strength and power.

When you read and see the word "God," say, "That's *Elohim*, the God of STRENGTH AND POWER—and He's my God!"

For in him all things were created: things in heaven and on earth, visible and invisible, whether thrones or powers or rulers or authorities; all things have been created through him and for him.

COLOSSIANS 1:16

EL ELYON

GOD MOST HIGH

I will give thanks to the LORD because of his righteousness;
I will sing the praises of the name of the LORD Most High.

PSALM 7:17

El Elyon is one of the most MAJESTIC names of God that we find in the Scriptures. It means "The God Most High" or "The Mighty One Most High," a name that carries great authority on your behalf.

I cry out to God Most High, to God, who vindicates me (Psalm 57:2).

EVERYTHING IN HEAVEN AND EARTH BELONGS TO HIM. *El Elyon* is a name that is untouchable in quality and incomprehensible in dominion and might. *El Elyon* is your SPIRITUAL AUTHORITY and He is your victory over anything that will ever cross your path.

For the LORD Most High is awesome, the great King over all the earth.

PSALM 47:2

First introduced in the book of Genesis, *El Elyon* comes from the root word *ālā*, meaning "TO GO UP, ASCEND, CLIMB, OR EXALT." It is a name that says there is no existing thing that is higher than the Most High God. He is the possessor of heaven, earth, and everything in them. His name is highly exalted, extravagant and marvelous. There is NO OTHER NAME to compare with His name.

El Elyon is so majestic that this was the name that Satan coveted for himself. EL ELYON IS ABOVE ALL EVIL, GREATER THAN ANY OTHER POWER.

NO MAN CAN CURSE WHAT GOD HAS BLESSED . . . HE ALWAYS HAS THE LAST WORD, AND THAT WORD IS "VICTORY!"

JEHOVAH

THE UNCHANGEABLE, INTIMATE GOD

The LORD replied, "My Presence will go with you, and I will give you rest."

EXODUS 33:14

Derived from the Hebrew word *chavah*, which means "to live," the name *Jehovah* is literally full of life! This name of God reveals His heart to have a PERSONAL RELATIONSHIP with His people.

But from everlasting to everlasting the LORD's love is with those who fear him, and his righteousness with their children's children . . . (Psalm 103:17).

The life of Moses is a perfect paradigm. From wandering in the wilderness, to the parting of the Red Sea, to the deliverance of the Israelites, Moses learned to OBEY AND TRUST *Jehovah* by walking closely with Him. Moses was determined to see the glory of God, and he did!

... *"I am the God of your father, the God of Abraham, the God of Isaac and the God of Jacob."*

EXODUS 3:6

God revealed Himself to Moses and the Israelites as *Jehovah*—the One Who never changes. He's THE SAME YESTERDAY, TODAY AND FOREVER.

Jehovah is the One Who is now and always has been. This is the God of life, THE GOD OF ETERNITY!

Declare what is to be, present it—let them take counsel together. Who foretold this long ago, who declared it from the distant past? Was it not I, the LORD? And there is no God apart from me, a righteous God and a Savior; there is none but me (Isaiah 45:21).

EVEN TODAY, JEHOVAH REVEALS HIMSELF AS YOUR INTIMATE, PERSONAL GOD.

JEHOVAH ROPHE

THE LORD, MY HEALTH

"'But I will restore you to health and heal your wounds,' declares the Lord . . ."

JEREMIAH 30:17

The name *Jehovah Rophe* actually means "*Jehovah* heals" or "*Jehovah* my Health." First used during one of the earliest situations the Israelites experienced in the wilderness, *Jehovah Rophe* was another way of God revealing His character and tender heart—He is your HEALER.

Praise the LORD, my soul, and forget not all his benefits—who forgives all your sins and heals all your diseases . . . (Psalm 103:2–3).

When the children of Israel arrived at Marah, they found a huge pool of water, but it tasted terribly bitter. The people began murmuring against Moses because they could not drink the water. Moses cried out to the Lord, and the Lord showed him a piece of wood and told him to throw it into the water. This act of OBEDIENCE AND FAITH turned the water from bitter to sweet (see Exodus 15:25–26).

The wood foreshadowed the cross and the healing that's available to believers today. CAST EVERY CARE ON JESUS. *Jehovah Rophe* has healing for your life—emotional, physical and spiritual. BRING EVERY HEARTACHE AND AFFLICTION that has wounded you to *Jehovah Rophe,* and allow Him to heal you.

Jesus went throughout Galilee, teaching in their synagogues, proclaiming the good news of the kingdom, and healing every disease and sickness among the people (Matthew 4:23).

JEHOVAH ROPHE
WANTS TO **CARE** FOR YOU,
HE WANTS TO **HEAL**
AND **MAKE YOU WHOLE!**

JEHOVAH JIREH

THE LORD, MY PROVIDER

"For I know the plans I have for you," declares the LORD, "plans to prosper you and not to harm you, plans to give you hope and a future."

JEREMIAH 29:11

Jehovah Jireh wonderfully enhances the meaning of *Jehovah's* name. It is the first compound name of God found in the Old Testament.

Jehovah Jireh first appears in GENESIS 22. It was revealed to Abraham when he faced perhaps the most difficult trial of his faith.

Abraham finally received his promised son, Isaac, from God, and now God asked Abraham to offer Isaac as a sacrifice. Yet, Abraham stood firm and didn't waver at God's request. HE KNEW GOD WOULD KEEP HIS PROMISE—even if that meant raising Isaac up from the dead.

Early the next morning Abraham got up and loaded his donkey. He took with him two of his servants and his son Isaac. When he had cut enough wood for the burnt offering, he set out for the place God had told him about.

GENESIS 22:3

If anyone speaks, they should do so as one who speaks the very words of God. If anyone serves, they should do so with the strength God provides, so that in all things God may be praised through Jesus Christ (1 Peter 4:11).

DOWN TO THE THE VERY LAST DETAIL, ABRAHAM WALKED IN OBEDIENCE.

When all of the preparations had been made, Abraham lifted his arm to slay his son when an angel of the Lord spoke to him. As he looked, right before his eyes, was a ram for the sacrifice.

GOD SAW AHEAD AND PROVIDED a sacrifice because He knew Abraham's heart and knew Abraham would trust His promise.

No temptation has overtaken you except what is common to mankind. And God is faithful; he will not let you be tempted beyond what you can bear. But when you are tempted, he will also provide a way out so that you can endure it (1 Corinthians 10:13).

After the ram had been offered up as a burnt offering of consecration, Abraham gave the place of sacrifice a name: *Jehovah Jireh,* "the revealing One Who is MORE THAN A PROVIDER."

EL SHADDAI

THE ALL-SUFFICIENT ONE

Whoever dwells in the shelter of the Most High
will rest in the shadow of the Almighty.

PSALM 91:1

The name *El Shaddai* is derived from the word "field," as in, "THE FIELDS PRODUCE ABUNDANCE." It is also translated as breast, or "the many-breasted One," which is a sign of nourishment and productivity. When you see the name *El Shaddai*, God is saying, "I am MORE THAN ENOUGH to meet your needs in every circumstance."

Abraham had no son to pass on his inheritance. When Abraham was 99 YEARS OLD, *El Shaddai* came to him and said, "I'll give you seed as as numerous as the stars in the sky and as the sand on the seashore." (See Genesis 22:17.) Adding to the difficulty of that promise, Abraham's wife, Sarah, was 89 YEARS OLD.

El Shaddai demonstrates God's ALL-SUFFICIENCY by turning nature around and providing miracles that are contrary to natural events. Since God Himself set the course of nature in motion, He is MORE THAN CAPABLE of intervening in natural events. The all-sufficiency of *El Shaddai* blessed Abraham and Sarah with a child in spite of their old age.

The Bible says that ABRAHAM'S BLESSINGS REST UPON EVERY BELIEVER, and those blessings are from *El Shaddai*. In the New Testament, you find Jesus fulfilling this promise by proclaiming, "I came to give you life in abundance!"

El Shaddai wants to be more than enough to you. SPEAK to Him. Get to KNOW Him, and TRUST Him as the all-sufficient One.

I will say of the LORD, "He is my refuge and my fortress, my God; in whom I trust" (Psalm 91:2).

"The thief comes only to steal and kill and destroy;
I have come that they may have life, and have it to the full."

JOHN 10:10

ADONAI

LORD & MASTER

*For the one who was a slave when called to faith in the Lord is the Lord's
freed person; similarly, the one who was free when called is Christ's slave.*

1 CORINTHIANS 7:22

Adonai is used more than 300 TIMES in the Old Testament alone, and it literally means "Master, Owner, or Lord." This name signifies ownership and indicates the PERSONAL RELATIONSHIP and responsibilities of being owned by God.

In the book of Exodus, the Bible says that the Israelites allowed slavery on a limited basis. If a man were so poor that he could not support himself financially—and was in danger of poverty and starvation—he could approach another Israelite and say, "Could I be your slave for six years?" As a slave, this man was responsible to OBEY every order, and his master would provide his food, lodging, direction and protection.

. . . *you were bought for a price.*

Therefore honor God with your bodies.

1 CORINTHIANS 6:20

In the seventh year, the slaves were allowed to go free, but if a slave decided to remain in slavery, the master would pierce his ear and plug the hole with the master's coat of arms or a special color. This was the slave's way of saying, "I am a slave by MY OWN CHOICE. I will never be free, and my master has obtained my total obedience for life."

Adonai is the God Who completely owns His people, but will protect them, provide for them and direct them. *Adonai* is the Master whose servants have chosen to serve Him BECAUSE THEY LOVE HIM. This is a beautiful illustration of the Father-Son relationship that exists between God the Father and Jesus the Son. JESUS CAME TO EARTH—BY THE FATHER'S WILL—TO REDEEM US.

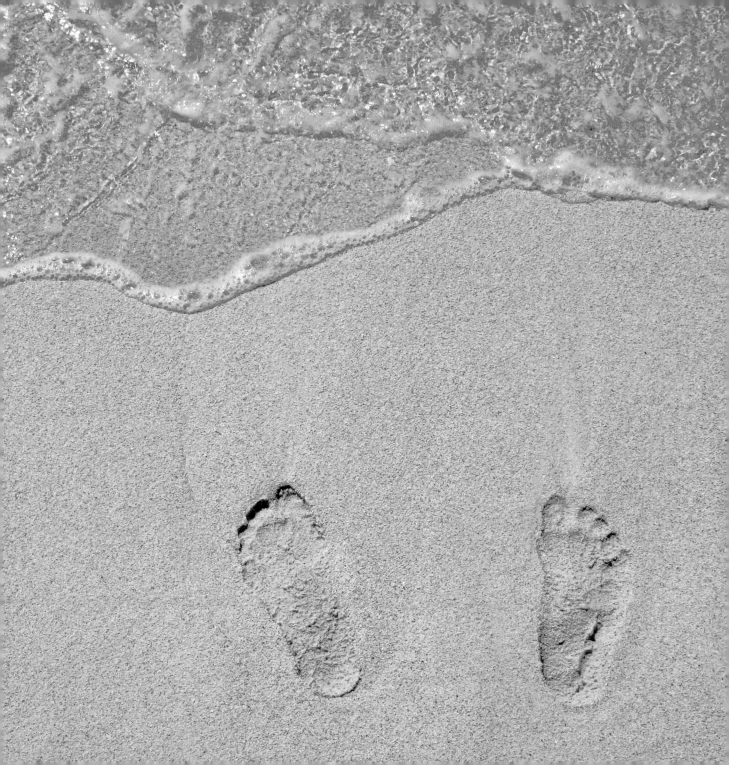

Now the Lord is the Spirit, and where the
Spirit of the Lord is, there is freedom.

2 CORINTHIANS 3:17

JEHOVAH ROHI

THE LORD, MY SHEPHERD

The LORD is my shepherd, I lack nothing.

PSALM 23:1

The name *Jehovah Rohi* means "JEHOVAH, MY SHEPHERD." The dominant meaning of the word *rohi* is "TO FEED." A second meaning of the word *rohi* suggests "the relationship between a prince or leader and his people." A beautiful translation of *rohi* is "COMPANION OR FRIEND." This translation communicates the idea of intimacy and sharing life and food—and certainly is characteristic of Jesus in His relationship with His disciples.

Jesus told Peter, in the book of John, "Feed my lambs . . . feed my sheep." The Good Shepherd was speaking to the "under-shepherd." Peter is a perfect reminder to us that WE'VE ALL GONE ASTRAY LIKE LOST SHEEP—but we return to Him Who is the Shepherd of our souls. Sheep lose their way quicker than almost any other animal, but when they go astray, a good shepherd notices and will search for them until they are safely in his care.

Jesus is not only the GOOD SHEPHERD, but He intimately knows His sheep because He too lived as a man; He understands the difficulties of life and knows firsthand how to lead and protect His sheep.

Jehovah Rohi's character is to lead you away from trouble, to sustain you in difficult times—to be **A SHEPHERD WHO KNOWS YOU BY NAME.** Sheep that follow the Shepherd become well acquainted with Him. They come to know His voice and His calling by spending time in His presence.

By knowing God as your *Jehovah Rohi*, **YOU CAN ALWAYS BE CONFIDENT ENOUGH TO SAY . . .**

*Surely your goodness and love will follow me all the days
of my life, and I will dwell in the house of the LORD forever.*

PSALM 23:6

SEVEN REVEALED NAMES

JEHOVAH SHAMMAH

GOD IS THERE

Jehovah Shammah means "*Jehovah* is there." This is the Lord's promise and pledge to His people that His presence will be with them.

JEHOVAH MAKKEH

THE LORD WHO MOLDS ME

The purpose of *Jehovah Makkeh,* "the Lord our Smiter," is to shape and perfect us into smooth, lively stones that are molded together to operate in unity.

JEHOVAH GMOLAH

THE LORD WHO REWARDS

Jehovah Gmolah is "the Lord of Recompenses." The meaning of the word "recompense" is "to repay, to reward, or to compensate."

JEHOVAH NISSI

THE LORD, MY BANNER OF VICTORY

When you hear the word "banner," you probably picture a flag, but a banner wasn't that in the days of Moses. It was often a bare pole with a bright and shiny ornament that would glitter in the sun when held high in the air, representing God's cause. When Moses stood at the edge of the Red Sea, the rod that he held in his hands was more than a mere rod. Moses was holding up the banner of God, which brought victory to Israel.

JEHOVAH SHALOM

THE LORD, MY PEACE AND WHOLENESS

The word *Shalom* is used 170 times throughout the Bible, and when translated, it simply means "peace." *Shalom* also means "whole." You are whole when God's peace reigns in your heart. David said in Psalm 16:6 that it is the heritage of God's children to have peace. The Lord will bless His people with peace in every possible situation.

JEHOVAH M'KADDESH

THE LORD, MY SANCTIFIER

The name *Jehovah M'Kaddesh* means "*Jehovah* who sanctifies." The verb "to sanctify" means "to consecrate, to dedicate, or to become holy." *Jehovah* sets His people apart to walk in holiness because He is their God. Consequently, The Lord's people were called to set themselves apart and walk in complete and total dedication to Him. Within the personality of *Jehovah M'Kaddesh* lies the truth that men must choose holiness.

JEHOVAH TSIDKENU

THE LORD, MY RIGHTEOUSNESS

Jehovah Tsidkenu means "*Jehovah*, our Righteousness." "Righteousness" means morally right. The world's religions are all attempts to make man "right" or good enough to be able to approach God. But in Jeremiah 23:5–8, God revealed Himself as "The Lord, our righteousness," reminding people that it's faith in Him and His ways that put you in right-standing with God.

I PRAISE YOUR NAME FOR YOUR UN-
FAILING LOVE AND FAITHFULNESS;
FOR YOUR PROMISES ARE BACKED BY
ALL THE HONOR OF YOUR NAME.

PSALM 138:2 NLT